SAUDADE

poetry by: Siri Svay

ISBN-13: 978-0-9996950-0-5

· THANK YOU'S ·

I would like to thank my family for their support, pushing me to chase the various dreams I've had and ultimately providing the black and white marble-patterned Mead journals to write down my innermost thoughts.

I would like to thank my friends for their support; the ears that listened to the live tellings of these poems and the hands that helped me through my darkest moments.

I would like to thank my readers for their support; those who have no obligation to me. Through these honest words, I hope to touch and connect with anyone going through hard times.

Just remember: no one is ever truly alone.

· TABLE OF CONTENTS ·

· ·

After a heavy rain,

flowers begin to bloom.

So after your tears of pain,

a new perspective looms.

· ·

PART I

ANGST.

Saudade

Introduction

Hello. My name is Siri Svay.
You might wanna be my friend, but I'd stay away.
Struggles and trouble seem to be inevitable with me,
so I don't know if that's where you wanna be.
I like making friends, so that's what I try to do.
Maybe my new best friend could possibly be you.
I'm friendly and that gets misinterpreted as flirtation,
but I'm told I'm one interesting and unique sensation.
Honestly my positivity is always down low,
and I fuck shit up, just thought I'd let you know.
I can be your best friend or your worst enemy.
I'm warning you now so you won't be surprised to see
my flaws are endless like millions of thread,
so much anxiety constantly runs through my head.
I try my hardest to hide everything in the shadows,
but I'm only human... so you know how that goes.

Sheltered

Why don't they understand
that I am growing up now
and I need my space?
Why must they reprimand,
forcing freedom to take a bow,
leaving resentment burning in my face?

Why am I locked up inside
and never allowed to go out there?
A prison instead of a warm shelter.
Why do I have to hide?
Innocence overprotected from being shared
when experiencing the world would be better.

Why must this be the way we live?
In fear of inevitable corruption.
We can't stay caged forever.
Why won't they allow any give?
Trying to control our every direction.
It's time to break free, fly and wander.

Privacy

A place for me.
My own space to be free
where I can be alone
that I can call my own.
Over my shoulder,
my stare gets colder.
I see you watching me
and my anger boils quickly.
With my every motion to your witness,
words I say could create a mess.
You constantly hover,
desperately trying to cover
tiny details from pointless questions,
but it only creates more tension.
I wanna scream and shout,
a burning desire to find a way out.
An escape from the misunderstood and misconstrued.
A private, enclosed space of solitude.

A Little Girl

Him and I, we are the same age,
but I feel like I'm stuck in a cage.

You treat him like he's an adult,
you allow him to play the games.
I know that this is not his fault,
but why don't you treat us the same?

I feel so misunderstood by you
'cause I'm never allowed to do
anything in the world.
I'm being treated like a little girl.

Why do you favor him like this?
You know that we are both fourteen,
but I am treated just like little kids.
And yet you treat him like he's eighteen.

Why do you say that I'm too young,
that I won't be able to understand?
Yet you tell him to go and have fun
without even a thought of reprimand.

Tired of being treated like a little girl.
I'm standing up for myself.
I'm gonna end this quarrel.
I'm getting off this shelf.

Sister Complex

She's the girl everyone wants to know,
the girl people follow everywhere she goes,
the girl who is always nice and super fun,
the girl most guys think, "She's the one."
She's so damn lovable, adorable, incredible.
She's the girl who always smiles,
the girl with her own unique sense of style,
the girl with the infectious laughter,
the girl that all the guys chase after.
She's so damn lovable, adorable, incredible.
She's the girl who's cute and funny,
the girl who makes a rainy day sunny,
the girl who brings the room to life,
the girl the guys want to make their wife.
I wish I was so damn lovable, adorable, incredible.

I Am Me

I've lived a double identity,
wearing two masks simultaneously.
One face that I call my own.
The other, a fake face for home.
The adult living her life freely,
yet a child living in secrecy.
You criticize my interests and career choice,
you like to hear your authoritative voice,
then you tell me what to do
like I'm under your control.
I try to be respectful to you
and not react like an asshole.
You don't like the way I dress or the way I wear my
hair,
but I'm twenty-one years old now and you really
shouldn't care.
You'll probably hate the music I listen to,
"Don't listen to that trash, it's bad for you."
I'd say that I'm sorry but I'm not.
I'm not my true self as you thought.
If only I could be the real me around you.
Now that would be a wonderful wish come true.

Losing Friends

Losing friends
is losing a part of me,
but friendships end
and who knows where they'll be.

You may not talk anymore,
and you're wishing you could again.
But as he's headed toward the door,
muster up the strength to let him go then.

She may not be moving far away,
but any distance can create a further divide.
You wish that she could stay,
so fight the uncertainty that burns inside.

These are the people you'll miss,
who turn into fond memories,
forever imprinted in bliss,
when you reminisce your beautiful histories.

Fifteen Minutes

I know you're craving it.
You keep replaying it.
You want to relive it.
You want to revive it.
That spotlight is your desire.
You want to feel that fire,
fire ignited by sparks,
sparks leaving your mark.
Your fifteen minutes of fame have gone by.
You're no longer the target of their eye.
You're yearning for the attention stay,
but it's a shame that it's going away.

Maiden's Intuition

She looks in the mirror and what does she see?
A sad, lonely maiden who is not worthy.
Beauty that never reaches the highest mountain,
always in jeopardy of being forgotten.
Thine eyes filled with hatred and jealousy
with hungry hands that tremble viciously.
A smile worn as the best disguise
with an intent malicious and unwise.
Her beloved, who is stubborn and clueless,
always speaks with a tone of the ruthless.
Concerned with saving thy skin and thy mistress,
he pushes the maiden further to breed loneliness.
Though he uses his ears, never his brain,
he seldom hears the maiden's pain.
The struggle of trust is no easy feat,
but the maiden feels compelled to compete,
because thy mistress has a special place in his heart,
and thy mistress is the one tearing them apart.

Mouse Trap

Like a mouse caught in a trap,
I always set myself up to fall in the gaps.
I know the consequences of what will happen,
yet I still fall for it over and over again.
I'm a troubled soul with a veil of happiness.
The act I put on every day as a covered up mess,
pretend that I'm happy when I'm really not,
it's much easier than I thought.
Life gives me occasional ups, but they don't sustain.
It's better than nothing; I shouldn't complain.
Fake smiles help you all not to worry
'cause I feel joy seeing you all happy.
I'm willing to put my selfish needs away
as long as I see your smiling faces every day.

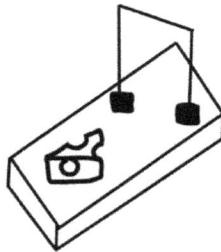

Erase the Past

What did I do?
Past actions of no good,
carrying a heavy guilt so strong
of all that I've done wrong.
Sometimes I just wanna erase the past,
wanting badly to take back what I did last.
Retract the angry words that I said,
rewind them back into my hot head.
I wanna forget and relive,
but will they forgive?
I promise not to be a burden.
Can we start over again?

Daily Thoughts of Anxiety

I hope I'm not gonna be late.
I slammed the door, whoops.
I hope no one heard that.
Someone probably woke up.
Where are my car keys?
Do I have enough gas?
What's traffic gonna be like this morning?
I have an hour and a half to get to the office.
Should I listen to music?
No, I might start singing and stop paying attention.
How about a podcast?
No, I might get too invested and stop paying attention.
It's 6am... how are there are so many people on the
road already?
I hope I'm not late.
Is this traffic going to clear up?
I have an hour 'til the office opens.
Traffic is backed up. What's happening?
Is there an accident?
Are any lanes closed?
How much longer 'til we move
again?
Did I miss my exit?
My GPS didn't tell me.
Thanks for not notifying me, GPS.
Now I might be late.
One-way streets are the worst.
I feel like I might turn onto one going the wrong way.
Why are these red lights taking forever?
I have to be in the office in ten minutes.
Why'd I miss the garage for the third time?!
I'm so incompetent.
I hate rushing.

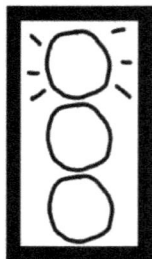

Now I have to run in these heels.
What floor am I going to?
Am I going the right way?
How do you people know which way to go?
I must look so completely lost.
Everyone is staring me.
Please stop looking at me.
I'm not from here.
I guess I can ask the receptionist...
Oh my God, this couple in front of me is taking their sweet time.
I have to be up there in five minutes.
Okay, this elevator ride is my last moment alone before I go up there...
Oh, there's a girl coming in the elevator with me.
And we're going to the same floor.
How awkward.
Do I smile? Do I say "hello?"
"Hi."
She smiles weakly.
Oh God, she hates me.
She gets off first.
We go into the same office.
"Can I help you?"
Uh... sweating. "I'm new."
I hope my trainee is nice.
I hope I can do this.
I can't mess this up.
I have to get this down.
I don't wanna look stupid.
Incompetent.
Unqualified.
Disappointing.
Let everyone down.
Ringing phones freak me out.

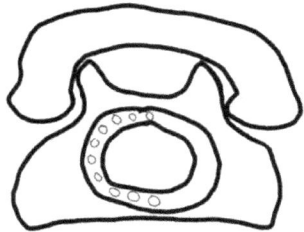

My heart jumps.
My lungs freeze.
I forget how to speak.
How do words work?
What do I say again?
What if the caller gets angry at me?
Because I'm incompetent.
I don't know if I can do this.
Why does my voice change when talking to people?
Can they tell I'm nervous?
Can they smell my fear?
Does my smile seem friendly enough?
Or do they know I'm hiding behind it?
Is it hot in here?
Why am I sweating?
Maybe I should drink some water.
No, 'cause I might have to pee...
I'd have to leave the desk.
I might miss calls or visitors.
Or worse! I might bleed into the chair.
Because of course my period started.
My first day on the job.
On Friday the thirteenth.
What a mess that'd be.
How embarrassing.
I'll wait 'til lunch break.
Holy moly! Everything in the office went from zero to
one hundred.
Quiet to chaos.
There are so many people.
Who do I help first?
Have they been assisted?
Are they ready to go?
Smile. Just smile.
Remain calm.

Phew.
How does everyone keep composure?
That was too much excitement.
I hate being alone.
Staring at the phone.
I hate surprises.
And every call that comes in scares me.
It's almost the end of the day.
The clock ticks slowly.
It mocks me.
To remind me to wait.
My legs shake.
It's a nervous habit.
Finally. Time to go home!
I hope I don't get lost getting out of the garage.
The garage is so small.
I hope my car doesn't scrape the concrete walls.
How does any other car fit through here?
Especially trucks.
They're so large.
How long's it gonna take to get home?
Is traffic bad?
Whyyyyy... is this guardrail so close to my car?
I'm going to hit it.
Then my car will ricochet
and hit other cars.
Then we cause a major
accident.
Then we tumble down, over
the freeway.
Crash.
AH! I have to stop imagining
the worst.
Focus.
I'm so close to being home.

Why is every road backed up?
I'm biting my nails.
I shouldn't, though.
This is why I can't ever paint my nails.
They're torn up, short and don't match lengths.
It's so ugly.
And now I'm bleeding.
Wow. Why do I do this?
There aren't any napkins in my car.
Lovely, I can bleed to death before reaching home.
Almost there.
Home.
I don't want to talk to people.
Answer the same questions.
I've hit my people interaction threshold.
I just wanna lay in my bed.
And close my eyes.
Rest.
I hope no spiders are hiding in my sheets.
There's always one on my pillow.
I slump up the stairs.
Avoiding any talking.
I open my door.
Stuff dropped on the floor.
And jump onto my bed.
Goodnight.

Siri Svay

Attention

We all crave it,
a feeling we can't live without,
a high we seek out all hours of the day,
a drug that masks our unwanted shadows.
Sweet candy perfection that we pine for,
but any bit is never enough.
After a moment in the spotlight, we want more;
more, more, more.
That constant admiration to validate ourselves,
that we are accepted,
that we stand out,
that we are beautiful,
that we are worthy.

Circles

I'm a robot,
daily routines every day.
Every second of life queued to the tee,
predictable and monotonous, nothing new.
Constantly running in circles,
chasing dreams that never come true.
No time, no money, nothing to contribute.
I'm sorry I don't have time or money to pursue.
Constantly fighting just to survive.
Maybe it's time to give up,
move on and accept fate,
that I will never stop working,
never meant to be someone.
I have nothing to show for my talents.
My words are all I have.
I'm getting nowhere,
just running in circles,
an endless road that leads to disappointment,
self-hate and loneliness.
What am I doing with my life now?
Chasing money instead of dreams.
I don't have time for dreams anymore.
If I wanna make it in the real world,
I can't do this life anymore.
I just wanna be numb,
not feel any of this pain,
not feel any of this struggle,
not feel any of this constant
battle.
I've lost faith;
faith in myself,
in my dreams,
in the future.

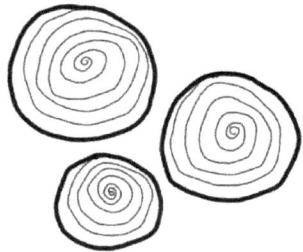

Saudade

I'm stuck in my ways,
a routine that never changes.
I don't know who I am;
just an insignificant nobody,
who thinks they can make it.
I miss home;
I long for it,
a haven where it's safe
with no worries about surviving.
I can be happy,
I can be alive;
I miss feeling alive,
I miss being passionate.
What happened to me?
I lost myself trying to be successful.

Used

It's unfair
how hard you work, but
you get the short end of the stick.
Bend over backwards with flexibility,
yet you get knocked down.
You're in a world where nepotism reigns.
Even when you've lied to protect them,
you get no recognition.
Nothing you do is good enough,
forever living in the bottom tier
and constantly fighting to get more stability.
They're a selfish mess, horrible at communicating.
Everyone busts their ass to make them successful,
and in return they go gallivanting
on endless trips around the world.
You've been walked all over and used before,
so now's the time to refuse to be wronged anymore.
Remember the bullshit you had to deal with.
Grow stronger, toughen your thick skin.
Even if they see you as nobody,
just know that you are somebody.

Jump Ship

Step by step the pain begins.
The line I walk is wearing thin,
fighting back tears welling in my eyes,
giving one last fight before goodbyes.
Never surrender, never give in;
the mantra they say to believe in.
But as hard as we try,
sometimes we have to scream a battle cry.
It's time to jump ship
before the boat rocks and dips,
holding tight to not drown in misery,
but this journey might be history.
Pulling me under the heavy tides,
there's nowhere left to hide.
Now I wanna wave that white flag.
It's time to surrender everything I have.
I thought I could weather the worst storms,
but every budding rose grows its thorns.

Temptation

Lingering in your ear,
whispering senseless lies,
calling to your fear,
killing logic 'til it dies,
temptation spreads venom
through your brain,
taking over your internal kingdom
and driving you insane.
It is Satan's spell controlling you,
pushing you to do things you don't wanna do
with remorse as the prize you win
for embracing this devilish sin.
With no hesitation you believe
the devil on your shoulder,
the siren with dissonant melodies,
making your heart grow colder.
Temptation seduces you into a bed of misery
where you'll be screaming for eternity.

PART II

DEPRESSION.

Saudade

Unlucky Girl

There's a fire inside I want to shine,
but it'll never come out 'cause I'm shy.
Life is constantly bringing me down.
Trapped in a string of endless bad luck,
I wanna do so much more in this town,
but I'm forever stuck in this rut.
I fall down, scrape my knee
every single day.
The same monotonous routine
I wish I could change.
Rarely do I smile and actually feel it.
Repeatedly getting the short end of the stick.
I'm a ghost floating, forgotten, unseen,
living in the background, behind the scenes.
Maybe a horoscope can help me get through the night,
a message in the stars that says everything will be all
right.
Someone wake me when it's all over.
Someone bring me a four-leaf clover.
I'm just your average, unlucky girl.

Yelling

Everything I do is always wrong.
I can't do anything right.
I worry all night long
that I will never see the light.
I'm sick of all this yelling.
It's messing with my head,
but I know it won't be stopping.
I should accept I'm always wrong instead.
How can I live my life
without making any mistakes?
It's going to be a constant fight
trying to overcome this heartache.
Every day I feel like crying
from harrowing yells driving me crazy.
They don't see that I'm trying
to do better and be someone worthy.

Used Guitar

An old guitar sitting in the corner collecting dust,
strings strung out and beginning to rust,
waiting endlessly to make a pretty sound,
but no one will take the time to strum around.
The guitar's sweet nature and chestnut skin,
that beautiful frame that draws them in,
she's weathered through the worst of days
but now only wishes that someone would stay.
Feel her neck, smooth and slender,
hug her body, nice and tender,
play C to A to G then E and D.
This poor guitar's been locked up lonely,
yearning to play that sweet song
she's been wanting to sing all along.
Let's face it, everyone's a player,
finding new guitars to replace her,
thinking the new ones are better.
Let's face it, everyone's a player.
Now they won't stroke her neck covered with dust,
strings so old, they're about to bust.
Nothing but a sad song out of tune,
lost faith that no one will return soon.
Nothing but a sad, ghostly guitar withering away,
hoping someone new will come and play.

Blame

Blame can be passed around
until ultimately,
its rightful place is found
when it lands on me.
Even after all that's happened,
when the fights have ended,
I'm responsible for
all of this and more.
The heartache,
the tears,
the lost trust,
the hurt.
My eyes have opened to reality,
accepting what's been brought upon me.
The truth that can't be changed;
that it's my fault of causing all this pain.
From this we'll forgive and learn,
but for now it's my turn to burn.

Radio Silence

She's standing in a room full of people,
feeling lonelier than an empty room.
Invisible to the passersby,
who see through her with glazed eyes.
She's reaching for her happy little pill,
her escape of numbing will.
Emotionless and complacent.
No more pain, hurt or sentiment.
She's sitting in radio silence,
watching the world in motion.
A spectator of life's events,
swaying with the waves of the ocean.

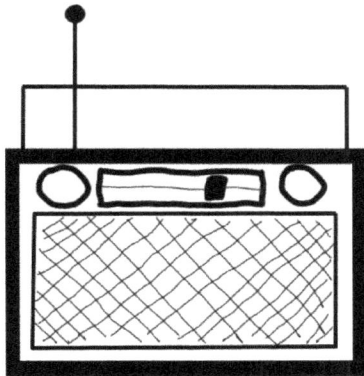

This Misery

How do I...
get by
this misery?
When did...
my life
get so crazy?
My world has turned upside down.
My world is spinning round and round.
Pain, heartache and tears
sustaining for years.
Who knew that one little thing
could cause this much spiraling?

Reset

I wanna feel numb.
I need that red serum,
bittersweet to coat my heart.
I'm sitting alone under the covers,
wishing I was someone other than me.
I'm contemplating my life choices and wonder
what things I could have done differently.
I'm not good enough, I never have been,
but all I want most is just to fit in.
Is it my turn yet to be a cool kid too?
I just wanna feel the high like they do.
I wanna laugh, basking in friends' warmth,
enjoying good times in company,
but instead I'm wandering in a heavy storm,
crying alone in silence and misery.
Sleepless nights with a running mind,
reminiscing memories, wasting time.
I need to find peace, a safe haven to escape.
Forget the world exists, only me in this place.
I wanna be happy,
an answer to my heart.
I need the push of a reset button for my life to restart.

Stubborn

I'm an addict,
constantly playing mind games by myself,
striving to be perfect.
A lone porcelain doll on the shelf.
I hate the reflection staring back.
I wanna break the mirror into a million shards,
shatter it so I see myself in the cracks,
all my insecurities unfolding like a house of cards.
I'm afraid to say what I want.
I have to hide all my skeletons that haunt.
I wanna scream but want no one to hear me.
Only the shadows lurking, keeping me company.
Break my silence, break my pride.
Is there anywhere I can hide?
I'm stranded in the dark depths of my mind,
spiraling thoughts choking me, leaving sanity behind.
So many hands to hold but I refuse to take them.
I'm in a shell, unable to open up and let anyone in.
So much misery, I'd rather suffer alone.
Tears leave their marks as I face the world on my own.
It's an obsession,
letting unhappiness take over me.
A selfish compulsion,
never setting myself free.

Signs

She's waiting for a sign,
a motion from the universe
to show her what's right.
You dancing thoughts, set her free.
End your necromancing indefinitely.
You spread like a deadly toxin
that she can't fight from within.
She puts a hand on the mirror,
reaching for who she wants to be.
Desire she can't ever possess,
an illusion in her reflection
to drive her mad and obsess.

Big White Room

Alone in a big white room,
four white walls enclosing me,
don't know how far each direction goes,
just wide open space of blank possibilities.
No sound except my beating heart;
it's the only conversation keeping pace.
Neither here nor there, close or far,
it echoes in this empty place.
A shattered mirror to avoid facing myself,
hollow memories filling this vacant shelf.
I can do whatever I want,
yet I choose to lay here,
giving into fear.
Too timid to let go, to scream, to shout,
to get these raw emotions out,
to release burning feelings I should share.
But into the white void I stare,
or I choose to cry.
No strength to even try
to stand up and shift.
I'd be happy if the world could stay static
'cause thinking is a dangerous high-risk, high-reward
game,
getting lost in my thoughts all the same.
So keep me in this peaceful solitude
where there's no room to disappoint, to fail, to fall
through.
Let's just lose track of time,
whether it's day or night,
or if I run out of rhyme,
I'll just say what sounds right.
Honestly, I should start to walk to find my way,
to find the bright of day.

Walk this blank canvas 'til a path forms.
Find the color in this white storm.
But right now this big white room is home for me,
a necessary quiet sanctuary.
Empty my mind with thoughtless thoughts;
be with myself 'cause I'm all I've got.

Nightmares

I woke up from a nightmare that put me in fear.
I woke up in a fatal shock followed by tears.
I jumped out of bed from the same nightmare.
How am I supposed to sleep when I'm this scared?
Was I dreaming or was it actually real?
I thought by now I would have healed.

Crutches

Try to distract yourself from your problems,
but you can't run away forever.
Maybe if you wear a smile
that you can temporarily mend the wounds altogether,
no one has to know
how many tears you've held back
from falling down your cheek.
You don't have to wear that strong façade
to show how you refuse to be weak.
Just swallow it down
and depend on yourself for what you need.

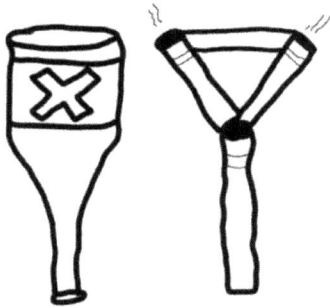

PART III

ANEW.

Saudade

Dear Jesus

Dear Jesus, I confess all of my sins.
There's filth underneath this skin.
Please guide me; tell me what to do.
It's time I confide in you.
Dear Jesus, I long to be happy.
There's an invitation for your light to shine upon me.
Please smile at me; fade away my fears.
It's time my pillows stop catching my tears.
Dear Jesus, your help is what I long for.
There's a welcome mat outside my door.
Please say you see what's in my heart.
It's time for me to make a new start.
Dear Jesus, will you answer my prayers?
There are no words to express my gratitude, my
savior.
Please accept this grateful praise.
It's time to repent and step out of the haze.

Be Strong

We have all been through,
we have experienced,
we have felt loss,
but life goes on.
We cannot break down,
we need to hold on,
we need to be strong,
and save our tears.
We can't let them fall,
we can't show fear,
we can't give in,
or let despair win.

Self-Love

I can see you've been in tears.
That's one of my worst fears.
I'll let you cry on my shoulder
and keep you from growing colder.
Dear, little darling, you can hush your cries.
I'm here for you to listen and be wise.
I'll comfort you 'til I see your smile.
Even if it takes a long while,
I'll take you in my arms and whisper in your ear
that everything will be okay from here.
It may not seem like it now 'cause times are bad,
but I'll be positive to keep you from staying sad.
Your dreams may have fallen through,
but I'm always here for you.
I can't bear to see you so down.
Just remember I'm always around.
I'm still here, your loyal friend.
Believe you will pick yourself back up again.

Hear Me

The passive voice is gone,
no longer going to be walked upon
and be the "yes" girl you're used to.
Now you're going to hear me
whenever I talk out loud.
Not going to hold my tongue,
not going to hide my feelings,
not going to reserve my face,
not going to quiet my mind.
The timid girl is gone
no longer going to be forced to do
things she doesn't wanna do.
Now I am flying free,
my own person with my own wings.
Not going back into the cage,
not going to forfeit autonomy,
not going to lock myself back up,
not going to revert to the past.

One More Year

One more year.
Be patient and it will be here.
The moment to venture to the next chapter
and be on my own thereafter.
I'm ready to be where I wanna be.
Be nobody else but me.
Not that person hiding behind closed doors,
pretending to be who everyone thought they knew
before.
My dreams are so close,
I can taste it on the tip of my tongue,
imagining the possibilities before they've begun.
Been waiting so long to get a taste of something real.
I wanna know what it's like to really live and feel.
Now's my time to shine;
you're truly gonna see me
not the girl you pressured me to be.
No more hiding behind tainted masks,
no more faking it.
This is my moment and I'm taking it.
Not gonna hold myself back anymore.
I can't wait to unleash what I've kept in store.
Been hiding what I've got to share with the world.
Now it's my time to let that unfold.

Running

I went for a run today.
Clear blue skies,
not a cloud in my mind.
The wind pushing me forward,
the concrete supporting every step,
taking me further away
from the person I was
and towards the person I wanna be.
Leave that old me behind,
forget all my regrets.
I'm not running away anymore
but rather, finding salvation,
a new change of heart,
a fresh start.

This City

See how the stars align just for me.
The city skyline is my rightful throne.
This is the view I've seen in my dreams.
I'm ready for this journey on my own.
See how the city scurries below,
even when night comes the city never sleeps.
This will forever be my stage, my show.
With all of my drive I take this faithful leap.
This is my home; where I'm supposed to be.
Working day and night without distraction,
I'm finally making my dreams reality.
This is me changing words into actions.
Watch as my kingdom glistens in the sunlight;
this city is my serenity.
For the moment right now, everything is right.
No one can take that away from me.
This city is my shining glory.
Watch me as I make my way to the top,
the beginning to my journey's story.
I'll keep climbing and won't ever stop.

Weather Predictions

I'm currently waiting for Autumn with its cool breeze.
I'm waiting patiently for the colorful leaves.
One leaf will fly with the wind and drift away,
saying goodbye to those it was close with in older days.
Another will turn red, slowly starting to fall,
dancing to the wind's siren, making its call.
A seed has been planted with the help of fate,
ready to blossom into something great.

Window

She thought she was looking through a window of
opportunity,
endless possibilities,
but she was staring at a mirror filled with demons
from her past
consuming her fast.
She wants to leave this old life behind;
find new adventure
discovering herself,
exploring new territory in the dark depths of her mind.
New memories for her,
not leaning on anyone else,
she needs a window of escape.
Outside where it's free,
ascending to a new place.
Outside where it's free,
saying farewell to the girl she once knew.
Outside where it's free,
then finally...
out the window she flew.

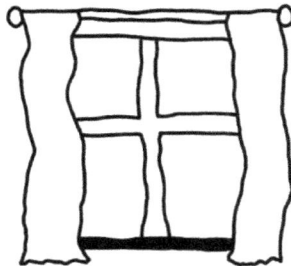

Life Anew

The dark hours have gone and passed.
Now you can open your eyes.
You've reached salvation at last.
No more happiness in disguise.
Recovery is not an easy road to walk on,
but I know you grow stronger every day.
Though the shadows are never truly gone,
I know you'll never let them stay.
You're one step closer today,
closer to the finish line.
Even though it always seems far away,
you'll get there in time.
You conquered the demons,
you can't even see them.
You can begin your life anew.
The struggle's been hard,
and even with the scars,
you made it through.

Open Road

Where do I wanna go?
There's nothing but open road.
Somewhere that takes me to the next chapter,
and who knows what will happen after.
I can't wait to see
all the adventures out there for me.
New, lively, profound places,
a sea of sun-kissed faces,
a destiny I've never known,
endless travels became my new home.

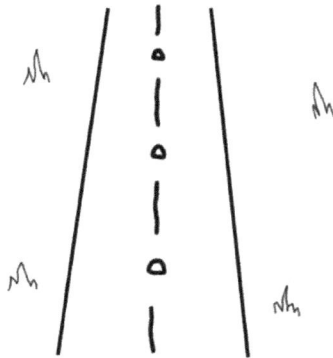

· ABOUT THE AUTHOR ·

Siri Svay is a writer who thrives on connecting with other people. Whether it's through personal relationships or the written word, Siri strives to relate to others on a deeper level. She strongly believes in sharing honest feelings and uses her life experiences as a platform of inspiration.

· STAY CONNECTED ·

www.sirisvay.com
www.twitter.com/sirisvay
www.instagram.com/sirisvay

Saudade is a collection of poems and prose derived from early days of teen angst to more recent tribulations of young adulthood.

The book is divided into three parts. It starts from everyday anxiety before diving into the lulls and heartaches that develop into depression, which is ultimately overcome and progresses into a new positive outlook of life anew.

www.ingramcontent.com/pod-product-compliance
Lightning Source LLC
Chambersburg PA
CBHW060536030426
42337CB00021B/4293